Out of the Dugout

ON BASE AND LEARNING:
EVERY KID, EVERY DAY.

Robert Kinghorn & Amy Thompson

CONTENTS

INTRODUCTION

WE ARE IN A PIVOTAL moment in the decades-long movement to make schools work well for all children. Although the goal to engage and empower all students has been at the heart of many school reform efforts, the digital tools to support this vision have taken on new relevance and urgency.

Out of necessity, educators around the world have learned the nuts and bolts of new digital platforms and tools. The pandemic has forced our profession into an unprecedented amount of professional learning. How will schools look as we decide which of these digital tools and practices will become integral parts of our work moving forward?

In order to make decisions that serve all students well, educators need a sturdy instructional framework. This book outlines an instructional framework for K–6 classrooms that will help teachers as they work to meet the needs of all learners through the purposeful use of technology.

During his five-year tenure as principal at a Title 1 school in Clearfield, Utah, Robert Kinghorn and the teachers working with him transformed the culture and raised academic outcomes, nearly doubling student proficiency rates on end-of-level state testing. Before this, Robert was part of the leadership team at a different turnaround school. They moved out of turnaround status in two years and created systemic change that has continued to this day.

For fourteen years, Amy Thompson worked as a classroom teacher at two Title 1 schools in Salt Lake City, Utah. During this time, both schools made remarkable gains in student growth and achievement. Amy likes to say she's never been as proud to receive a "B", which both schools earned for the first time on the state school evaluation system. Amy has also spent time as a special education teacher, as an instructional coach, and as an assistant principal.

During the 2019–2020 school year, we worked together as the new administrative team at a Title 1 school. We wove together our own experiences and understanding of best classroom practices with the work of supporting an amazing, committed staff. Through this work, we developed the *Out of the Dugout* instructional framework. With a set of shared language and clear priorities, we were able to support teachers as we refined instructional practices and moved toward more digitally integrated, project-focused classrooms.

This framework ended up being critical to our transition to the crisis remote teaching during the spring of 2020 and to hybrid teaching during the fall of 2021. Our faculty knew how to create meaningful learning experiences with digital tools, and we continued to see remarkable student growth throughout the 2020–2021 school year.

The instructional framework described in this book is based on our own experiences as educators and instructional leaders who have worked alongside many talented teachers. This framework is also based on several sets of ideas and research that have been part of the national education reform efforts of the last two decades.

Our aim is to give educators a simple, clear model that integrates a large set of best practices into a single framework with the intentional aim of helping all students become expert learners.

CHAPTER 1

Out of the Dugout

"**H**AVE A GREAT WEEKEND! SEE you Monday," we said to our students on Friday, March 13, 2020.

As the principal and assistant principal at a school in northern Utah, we spent most afternoons outside of our school building, saying goodbye to our five hundred elementary students. On that Friday in March, we also chatted with teachers as cars and buses pulled away. We all headed back into the building for our weekly Professional Learning Community meetings. Later that afternoon, we learned that our state was immediately closing all schools and that we would have the weekend plus two school days to prepare for emergency online teaching.

The next three months were a blur of challenges and problems that we could not anticipate from one day to the next. We checked out hundreds of devices, we learned how to Zoom, and we created lessons that students could access remotely. We scrambled, improvised, and fumbled as we adjusted to the limitations of remote instruction. We listened and responded to the concerns and needs of struggling parents. Many of us had our own children at home and faced the impossible demands of supporting them while also providing remote instruction to our students.

Although different regions of the United States brought students back to in-person learning at different times and with different models, the 2020–2021 school year continued to stretch and challenge all of us.

We learned how to provide instruction to in-person and remote students simultaneously. We learned how to support kindergarten students as they used learning management systems originally designed for college students. We found ways to assess and provide feedback from a distance. We learned how to give students safe ways to socialize and collaborate. As colleagues, we found new ways to support one another professionally, emotionally, and socially.

As a nation, on a much larger scale, all of us became acutely aware of the many inequalities in our schools and communities. Students were not impacted equally by the disruptions of the pandemic, as unequal access to technology and academic gaps have been laid bare.

We have all survived an incredibly challenging time period. As we move out of the crisis of the pandemic and start looking at the widespread return to in-person learning, we have an incredible opportunity. We need to understand and decide what the pandemic has meant for us, both personally and professionally.

In response to extreme stress and trauma, psychologists have documented the surprising prevalence of post-traumatic growth. Sometimes alongside and sometimes without the presence of post-traumatic stress, post-traumatic growth is a set of positive psychological changes that can occur as a result of trauma. Psychologists have identified several domains of post-traumatic growth (Collier, 2016).

The three domains that apply directly to our work as educators are an awareness of new possibilities, closer relationships, and a recognition of our own strengths. As we grapple with the losses and grief of the pandemic, we can also look for and foreground the many ways that we have experienced and can continue to experience positive growth.

One of the ways we have grown within our profession is with our flexible, creative, and purposeful use of digital learning tools. How will these new tools and skills shape our teaching practices going forward? As we integrate our recent experiences and our new technical skills into our pre-pandemic habits and routines, which tools and practices are worth keeping? How do we want our schools to be different? How do we want them to be the same?

Classroom teachers make about 1,500 decisions per day (Cuban, 2011). In addition to the decisions involved in planning and teaching lessons, teachers also make choices based on how students respond. Who needs today's content retaught? Who needs a few extra opportunities to practice a skill? Is there a lesson that is not part of the planned curriculum that the whole class needs tomorrow?

The combination of in-person and remote teaching has added new layers of complexity to our decisions. What is essential to do with students when we have the opportunity to meet in person? What can students learn to do independently? What are the benefits of paper, pencils, and physical books? How do we create positive, effective partnerships with caregivers?

When we have a long-term, big-picture vision and can also see how this vision connects to specific teaching practices, we become more confident, flexible, and resilient. These connections help us become skilled designers of student learning experiences. We can make better decisions about how to use and evaluate digital curriculum and tools. We can clearly communicate our decisions and advocate for resources. And, finally, we can organize and prioritize our own time, focusing on work that supports our long-term goals for students.

THE OUT OF THE DUGOUT MODEL

During each inning of a baseball game, two teams rotate between batting and fielding. The team that is on the field includes the pitcher, the infielders, and the outfielders. Meanwhile, the team that is up to bat sits in the dugout, while each player takes their turn getting up to bat.

Imagine that our students are the team that is sitting in the dugout, taking turns at bat. As students learn, they are getting up to the plate, hitting the ball, rounding the bases, and scoring runs. But unlike baseball, where players are required to sit in the dugout, waiting for their turn at bat, we can design classrooms where each student is constantly getting up to bat and rounding the bases of learning.

Getting every student out of the dugout and continuously engaged in "just right" learning activities is the central challenge of running an effective classroom. How can we meet the needs of each one of our twenty-plus students?

When educators integrate digital tools and move to more personalized, learner-centered practices, we can keep all students engaged and learning throughout each day. As they master new concepts and skills, as they work on open-ended projects, and as they set and meet goals, students are constantly getting up to bat and rounding the bases of learning. Instead of sitting on the bench in the dugout, students spend their days actively engaged, learning new knowledge and skills.

SUMMARY

In this book, we hope to provide an inspiring vision, common language, and concrete steps to realize the goals of digitally integrated, project-focused schools, where all students become expert learners. We hope this will be the beginning of many conversations and will serve as a way to turn the painful and difficult challenges of the pandemic into rich and productive opportunities for growth.

REFLECTION QUESTIONS

How has the pandemic changed your perspective on relation-ships—with colleagues, with students, with caregivers? _____

_____

_____

_____

_____

What are some of the new digital tools you have learned? How do you envision using these digital tools moving forward? ____

_____

_____

_____

What might an ideal blend of digital and traditional learning look like for you and your students?_____

_____

_____

_____

_____

REFERENCES

Cuban, L. (2011, June 16). Jazz, basketball, and teacher decision mak-ing. *Larry Cuban on School Reform and Classroom Practice*. https://larrycuban.wordpress.com/2011/06/16/jazz-basketball-and-teacher-decision-making/

Collier, L. (2016, November). Growth after trauma. Monitor on psy-chology. *The American Psychological Association*. https://www.apa.org/monitor/2016/11/growth-trauma

CHAPTER 2

Home Plate:
Every Kid, Every Day

IN ORDER TO CATEGORIZE, CLARIFY, and organize our thinking about the learning experiences we want to build for students, we start with a clear vision of our big-picture purpose and goals in K–6 schools. What type of learners do we want our sixth-grade students to be when they move on to secondary school?

A clear portrait of exiting sixth graders is at the center of this instructional framework. We call this vision the "home plate" of our framework. When they leave us, we want every one of our sixth graders to be expert learners. This means they have the knowledge, skills, and mindsets to drive their own learning. They are empowered learners who are prepared to take on the academic and social challenges of secondary school. They have had many opportunities to round the bases of learning. They are self-directed learners who don't wait in the dugout.

We call this vision the "home plate" of our framework to remind ourselves that this ambitious goal is for every student, and it's something we work for every day. It is a long-term vision that motivates and shapes our work. This is connected to a famous speech given by the legendary baseball coach, John Scolinos.

Coach Scolinos was a speaker at a gathering of coaches at a convention in 1994. He came on stage wearing a home plate around his neck. After talking for several minutes, Coach Scolinos finally acknowledged the home plate he had been wearing since coming on stage. John Sperry was in the audience that day and this is his account of the rest of the speech.

"You're probably all wondering why I'm wearing home plate around my neck. Or maybe you think I escaped from Camarillo State Hospital," Scolinos said, his voice growing irascible. I laughed along with the others, acknowledging the possibility. "No," he continued, "I may be old, but I'm not crazy. The reason I stand before you today is to share with you baseball people what I've learned in my life, what I've learned about home plate in my 78 years."

Several hands went up when Scolinos asked how many Little League coaches were in the room. "Do you know how wide home plate is in Little League?" After a pause, someone offered, "Seventeen inches," more question than answer.

"That's right," he said. "How about in Babe Ruth? Any Babe Ruth coaches in the house?"

Another long pause.

"Seventeen inches?" came a guess from another reluctant coach.

"That's right," said Scolinos. "Now, how many high school coaches do we have in the room?" Hundreds of hands shot up, as the pattern began to appear. "How wide is home plate in high school baseball?"

"Seventeen inches," they said, sounding more confident.

"You're right!" Scolinos barked. "And you college coaches, how wide is home plate in college?"

"Seventeen inches!" we said, in unison.

"Any Minor League coaches here? How wide is home plate in pro ball?"

"Seventeen inches!"

"RIGHT! And in the Major Leagues, how wide home plate is in the Major Leagues?"

"Seventeen inches!"

"SEV-EN-TEEN INCHES!" he confirmed, his voice bellowing off the walls. "And what do they do with a Big-League pitcher who can't throw the ball over seventeen inches?" Pause. "They send him to Pocatello!" he hollered, drawing raucous laughter.

"What they don't do is this: they don't say, 'Ah, that's okay, Jimmy. You can't hit a seventeen-inch target? We'll make it eighteen inches, or nineteen inches. We'll make it twenty inches, so you have a better chance of hitting it. If you can't hit that, let us know so we can make it wider still, say twenty-five inches.'" (Sperry, 2016)

Scolinos went on to tie the constant size of home plate to the importance of upholding high standards related to personal integrity and character. The take-away message: don't widen the plate!

For our purposes, we define home plate as the knowledge, skills, and mindsets that students need to develop to become expert learners. These are our non-negotiable student outcomes. All of our work is aimed at this single long-term goal. We will not widen the plate. We will provide every student with the knowledge, skills, and mindsets to become an expert learner.

This home plate, at the center of our framework, is held in place by our deep and strong commitment to our students' long-term trajectories. Expert learners become adults with many options to live productive, fulfilling lives.

What does an expert learner look like as an adult? Here's a true story from Amy's brother.

> At age twenty-nine, Kevin had a dream to become a physical therapist. His bachelor's degree was in the arts, so before applying to a physical therapy program, he had to take several advanced math and science classes.
>
> During the first weeks of his organic chemistry class, Kevin realized he was in trouble. Reading the textbook and attending traditional lectures were not helping him learn

the material. Organic chemistry is often used by colleges and universities to sort students, to weed out those who aren't up for the rigor and challenges of the health sciences.

Kevin saw that he wasn't going to pass the class without a different approach. "I realized that somehow I was going to have to learn it on my own," he said. As a first step, he went to the tutoring sessions provided by his college. One of the teaching assistants recommended that he try Khan Academy.

"Khan saved me," Kevin says now. "Sal Khan explained each concept carefully, simply, and clearly. I could pause a video and work out practice problems. I could check myself as I went. I could re-watch any video, anytime."

What started as Sal Khan's personal tutoring service for his own cousins has grown into one of the most widely used adaptive, personalized learning platforms. It provides free courses for students from preschool through college and has served millions of students around the world.

Founded on the belief that all people can learn, Khan's vision is to "provide a world-class education to anyone, anywhere." Khan Academy is centered around two of the highest effect-size variables in education: teacher clarity and feedback (Hattie, 2016).

When students enroll in Khan Academy, they have access to thousands of videos that explain thousands of discreet concepts. The videos are concise, brief, and clear. They are organized into courses with practice problems, quizzes and tests, which require students to thoroughly master each concept so that future related concepts are always built on solid ground.

Kevin earned an A in organic chemistry, received a scholarship to his physical therapy program, and in the spring of 2020, he was working in one of the hospitals in Manhattan that was severely impacted by Covid-19. He was part of a team that pivoted several times during the crisis. They adjusted and readjusted to respond to new needs and new information. Kevin is an expert learner who helps save lives.

Expert learners, who leave elementary school prepared to continue their growth in secondary school and beyond, need a specific set of knowledge, skills, and mindsets. What are the specific things that expert learners need to know and be able to do? What mindsets are important to cultivate? The rest of this chapter will look at these three questions in greater detail.

Knowledge – What do expert learners know?

When elementary students learn new concepts and information about the world, they are building scaffolding upon which future knowledge will continue to be built (Wexler, 2020). Each new definition and each link between related concepts are part of a growing web of understanding. A sturdy foundation of knowledge is crucial, and it is our responsibility to ensure our students move on to secondary school with this firm groundwork.

Expert learners acquire new knowledge and vocabulary through both printed texts and oral language. One way they access oral language is through digital media. Before they have acquired strong reading skills, students are able to learn complex words and ideas through videos and oral instruction. Kindergarten students can learn the meaning of words and can understand concepts that are far beyond their reading abilities. Fifth and sixth grade students, on the other hand, can acquire new word meanings and conceptual knowledge from print. Teaching elementary students involves fine tuning this balance between video, oral, and print materials as students mature.

Core Standards are the best guide for the specific content knowledge students need at each grade. Most states have adopted the Next Generation Science Standards, enabling US educators to collaborate with colleagues around the country as we teach science concepts. Most districts also have social studies standards that include introductory state, national, and global history curricula because students need a solid grasp of the historical and contemporary social concepts that will be referenced in secondary school and beyond. We can teach multiple perspectives and cultures while also giving students a solid foundation of knowledge about history, government, civics, and economics.

Knowledge is the Velcro upon which future knowledge sticks. When our students move on to secondary school, we want them to know how to access and evaluate information online. But in order to integrate and understand new ideas and concepts, students need to have a strong background of prior knowledge.

Knowing how to use google is an important skill. But this skill assumes that you know what to google in the first place. It also requires enough vocabulary words and conceptual relationships to understand the information that google delivers. It takes a foundation of knowledge to learn and understand new knowledge. You have to already know the meaning of many words and understand many concepts in order to both locate and understand new information when you look it up. A solid grasp of many words and concepts is also the foundation of our ability to understand what we read and hear and to efficiently acquire new knowledge.

Knowledge matters, and we are committed to ensuring our students are well prepared with a solid foundation of words, concepts, and ideas.

Skills – What do expert learners know how to do?

If knowledge is the set of vocabulary, concepts, and relationships that expert learners can define and discuss, what are the things that expert learners are able to do? Knowledge, alone, is not enough to become a student who is prepared for the demands of the twenty-first century. Expert learners also need to develop a specific set of academic skills.

In 2002, the Partnership for 21st Century Learning was founded to start a national conversation around the skills required for students to be prepared for the jobs of the twenty-first century. This coalition of business, education, and policy leaders identified the Four Cs as the learning competencies most critical for twenty-first century learners: collaboration, communication, critical thinking, and creativity.

Out of these national and international conversations came several new instructional approaches. Project-based learning (PBL) is a teaching and learning method that encourages the purposeful integration of real-world problems. Inquiry-based instruction is focused on eliciting student questions, which lead to guided investigations. Although STEM, by definition, is a curriculum focused on science, technology, engineering, and math, it is also an approach that prioritizes the practices that are central to these disciplines. These include skills like designing solutions, testing hypotheses, and developing new tools and models to represent complex data.

It is easy to get lost and overwhelmed while sifting through the jargon, acronyms, and priorities of these multiple, beneficial approaches. Yes, of course, we want to foster and grow the Four Cs. We want students who are creative and collaborative, who can ask questions, think critically, and communicate effectively. We want to ensure that our students will one day be prepared for the jobs of the future. But where and how do we start?

In 2013, Tina Cheuk created a three-circle Venn diagram mapping out the core practices of the Common Core Standards for Math and Language Arts, along with the core practices identified in the Next Generation Science Standards (Loewus, 2014). The overlapping sections of the three circles represent the practices or skills that math, English Language Arts, and science have in common. It turns out that there are many overlapping skills in these three core subjects.

In order to both simplify and clarify our goals for both ourselves and our students, we have identified six core thinking skills that represent these overlapping practices. If we design learning experiences with these six skills as guideposts, we will grow learners who can communicate effectively, create independently, and solve complex problems. They will also have the skills to *do* math, science, and ELA work at deep, advanced levels.

Here are the six core thinking skills:

Ask Questions

Build New Knowledge

Design Solutions

Communicate With Others

Create Models

Conduct Experiments

Using the Out of the Dugout model, teachers post these six core thinking skills in the classroom and teach them to students. Although this looks different in each grade, we teach students to describe how their daily work is connected to these specific skills and how to recognize their own growth.

As we plan, teach, and evaluate learning experiences, we keep the six core thinking skills in focus. We ask questions like:
- *Are my students learning to solve problems?*
- *Are my students learning new strategies to generate thoughtful questions?*
- *Can each of my students identify both a topic they are studying and at least one core thinking skill that they are working to improve?*

In chapter four, we will revisit these six thinking skills, looking at how we can foster their development throughout a student's elementary school years.

Mindsets – How do expert learners approach learning?

In addition to knowledge and skills, students in elementary grades also learn and develop mindsets. A mindset is a set of beliefs that are enacted when we are in a specific situation.

The feelings–thoughts–actions triangle is a helpful model for explaining the strong and powerful connections between how we feel, how our beliefs shape our thoughts, and how we act. Healthy mindsets shape our beliefs and thoughts, which influence both our feelings and actions in positive ways.

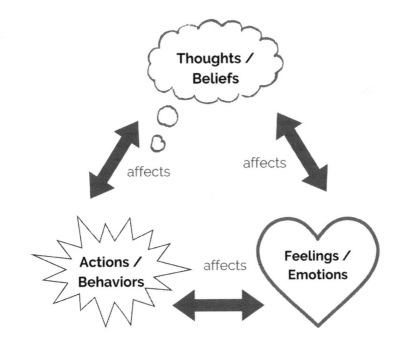

When using the Out of the Dugout method, the three mindsets that we deliberately work to cultivate in students are growth, belonging, and agency.

GROWTH – "I CAN LEARN ANYTHING."

In 2006, Carol Dweck published *Mindset, The New Psychology of Success.* This research and its implications have spread widely throughout education, and most teachers are familiar with the underlying concepts. In 2012, Dweck defined both growth and fixed mindsets.

> "In a fixed mindset, students believe their basic abilities, their intelligence, their talents, are just fixed traits. They have a certain amount and that's that, and then their goal becomes to look smart all the time and never look dumb.
>
> In a growth mindset, students understand that their talents and abilities can be developed through effort, good teaching, and persistence. They don't necessarily think everyone's the same or anyone can be Einstein, but they believe everyone can get smarter if they work at it."

In our daily work, there are three things that teachers can do to promote growth mindsets. First, teach students the brain science of learning. Even young students can learn about neurons, (brain cells) and synapses (the connections between neurons). We can teach kids that synapses get stronger when we practice, when we make mistakes, and when we work through challenges.

Second, we can foster growth mindsets through our language. Use specific feedback and praise students' efforts and strategies. Model what it looks and sounds like to have a growth mindset and to be a lifelong learner. Don't say things like, "I can't draw," or "I've never been good at math."

One teacher, who was working to develop better habits with her growth mindset language and praise, made this cheat sheet, which she reviewed twice each day.

> **Things to Say:**
> *You worked so hard!*
> *You kept going when it was challenging today.*
> *That's the feeling of your brain getting smarter.*
> *You used [name specific strategy] here...did this work? Why?*
> *Tell me more...*
> *Help each student say and believe: "I can learn anything.*

The third way teachers can help students develop growth mindsets is by making assessment and feedback focused on visible growth rather than on final grades, points, or fixed endpoints. We can use student-friendly learning targets, success criteria, and learning progressions to help students see where they are and where they are headed. If we believe the purpose of school is to help students learn and grow, we need to make our assessments and feedback into tools that promote learning and growth.

BELONGING – "I AM AN IMPORTANT PART OF A TEAM."

Belonging is the set of beliefs that are connected to how students see themselves in relation to various groups. In the Out of the Dugout model, we are intentional about helping each student develop a sense of belonging connected to their classroom and also to their school. School mottos, mascots, and mantras go far in fostering this sense of belonging at the school level. Morning meetings, check-ins, and using "we" and "us" language are ways to develop this mindset in each classroom.

When students have a sense of belonging and know that they are valued in a classroom community, they are willing to set ambitious goals, take risks, and solicit feedback. These are vital actions required for learning new skills.

There are several ways to create a positive learning community. Explicitly establish norms. Teach social skills, including respectful communication and problem solving. Model inclusive language, patience, and flexibility. Finally, enforce the rules that protect students' emotional safety. When students feel that they are a valuable part of a safe, supportive community, they are able to learn, grow, and thrive.

AGENCY – "I CAN SUCCEED!"

Agency is the mindset that captures the set of beliefs around selecting and achieving goals. Students need to believe they are capable of setting and achieving both short- and long-term goals. In order for this mindset to develop, students need many opportunities to make choices and to learn from both their effective and less-effective choices.

This mindset develops slowly throughout a student's elementary school years. Kindergarten and first grade students can make and set goals, but they need far more support than fifth and sixth grade students, who have developed a more mature ability to select goals and monitor their own progress.

In addition to providing students many opportunities to self-direct and reflect, teachers can also empower students to become better at accomplishing their goals by explicitly teaching them both goal setting and help-seeking strategies.

SUMMARY

As we plan lessons, design our daily schedule, evaluate student progress, and create a classroom learning environment, it is helpful to have a clear understanding and vision of what we hope this daily work will eventually lead to for each of our students. Are we growing expert learners who can independently acquire new knowledge and skills? Do our learning environments support the growth, belonging, and agency mindsets?

Shifting to a more learner-centered model can be uncomfortable. When we give students more independence, we might feel a loss of control. The home plate reminds us that these changes are worth it. When we imagine our current students as empowered, confident sixth graders, ready to move up to the next league of their education, we will continue to align our daily work with this vision.

But how do we do this? What does it look like? In the next chapter we'll take a close look at playlists, the main structure that we use to organize student learning and foster all of our home plate goals in the Out of the Dugout model.

REFLECTION QUESTIONS

What do you see as the home plate, or the set of non-negotiable outcomes, for the learners in your school or setting?

_____

_____

_____

_____

_____

How are knowledge, skills, and mindsets related to each other?

_____

_____

_____

What are some goal-setting strategies you have effectively used in your own life or with students? _____

_____

_____

_____

_____

REFERENCES

Wexler, N. (2020). *The knowledge gap: The hidden cause of America's broken education system—and how to fix it.* Avery Publishing.

Dweck, C. S. (2016). *Mindset: The new psychology of success.* Ballantine Books.

Sperry, J. (2016, December 9). "Stay at 17 inches." *Baseball/Life. https://www.sperrybaseballlife.com/stay-at-17-inches/*

Loewus, L. (2014, October 1). "Finding overlap in the common math, language arts, and science standards." *Education Week.* https://www.edweek.org/teaching-learning/finding-overlap-in-the-common-math-language-arts-and-science-standards/2014/10

Morehead, J. (2012, June 19). "Standford University's Carol Dweck on the growth mindset and education." *OneDublin.org.* https://onedublin.org/2012/06/19/stanford-universitys-carol-dweck-on-the-growth-mindset-and-education/

CHAPTER 3

Playlists

HOME PLATE IS WHERE EACH student is headed. To become expert learners, students need to grow a large base of knowledge, they need to become competent with each of the six core thinking skills, and they need to develop healthy mindsets that support learning. But how do we actually foster these long-term outcomes in our daily work as teachers?

To reach these specific outcomes, students need daily learning experiences that meet several criteria. To grow student agency and independence, we need to provide meaningful choices. We also need to give students many opportunities to practice each of the six core thinking skills. Students need to be actively designing solutions, creating models, conducting experiments, and communicating with others. And as if that isn't enough to take on, we also need to ensure that each student is spending their time on learning tasks that are not too easy or too difficult.

We like to compare this age-old teaching challenge to the classic Abbott and Costello comedy routine "Who's on First?" Here's a short clip.

Costello: And you don't know the fellows' names?

Abbott: Well, I should.
Costello: Well, then who's on first?
Abbott: Yes.
Costello: I mean the fellow's name.
Abbott: Who.
Costello: The guy on first.
Abbott: Who.
Costello: The first baseman.
Abbott: Who.
Costello: The guy playing—
Abbott: Who is on first!

The comedians go on to banter not only about the fellow named Who, but also about What, the player on second base, and Mr. I Don't Know, the guy playing third.

As teachers, we are constantly working to keep track of who is on each base. We have some students who start the year on first base, who are at a beginning level relative to grade-level standards. We also have some students who start on second base. And we usually have a handful who start on third base that zip around the bases with ease. How do we keep all of our students out of the dugout and meet the diverse needs of our twenty-plus unique learners?

Underlying this focus on the current skills of each learner is a theory that was developed by Lev Vygotsky in 1931. Vygotsky defined the Zone of Proximal Development (ZPD) as the set of skills that students can do with limited support, the things they can almost do independently.

As educators, we are constantly looking for ways to keep students in this sweet spot of learning. We want them performing tasks that are not too easy or too difficult. How do we keep each one of them in their Zone of Proximal Development throughout most of each school day?

Playlists are a way to organize a mix of digital and face-to-face learning that meet all of the criteria we've outlined (Tucker, 2020). Playlists are a flexible and versatile tool that students and teachers throughout a school community can use to develop the knowledge, skills, and mindsets of expert learners. Through online learning management systems, playlists can be shared with parents or caregivers who can support students in their individual progress. Here are three examples of playlist outlines that span the elementary grades and content areas.

How does light affect the growth of plants?	
Watch and Take Notes	Links to a series of three videos about the needs of plants. Students follow a template for taking notes that highlights key vocabulary and concepts.
Read and Research	Digital resources and physical books are provided for students to learn more about how plants grow. Students ask and answer their own questions. Books are at a variety of reading levels. Students report on their findings in physical or digital notebooks.
Experiment	Students plan an experiment to investigate the effect of light on plant growth. Over the course of two weeks, students document and analyze the results of their experiment.
Explain	Students create short videos explaining their experiments and their findings.

Why do we build and visit national monuments?	
Create	Students choose a tool to create a model of one specific national monument that they research in depth. They can build their models in Minecraft, with LEGO sets, or they can draw a 2D model.
Explain	Students write short essays about the history and meaning of the monument they have researched and modeled.
Gallery Walk	Students visit each other's monuments, and the teacher facilitates a whole class discussion on the purpose and meaning of national monuments.

How do I use a slide presentation to effectively communicate instructions?	
Tutorial	Students self-pace through a series of short videos as they create their own slide presentation about a self-selected pro tip.
Peer Feedback	Students post their presentations in a shared digital space and provide feedback for each other.
Reflect	Students reflect on their developing skills with the digital presentation tool and anticipate ways they can use the tool in the future.

Teachers will immediately recognize that there are many subskills embedded in these playlists that their students will need to be taught. We wouldn't assume, for example, that all second graders know how to get started asking and answering their own research questions. Some students will need sentence stems to support their writing. We can differentiate for the needs of learners as we anticipate these needs and prepare scaffolds and support tools.

All students will benefit from a clear learning progression that they can use to assess their current levels and see the precise next steps they can take to move toward stronger writing and speaking skills. Designing a playlist includes preparing for a variety of student learning needs.

As we design project-focused playlists, there are three things that we can do to foster our home plate outcomes more effectively: plan low floor, high ceiling tasks; make space for choice and voice; and teach toward independence. Deliberately and intentionally considering and including these three elements will help keep students out of the dugout, and in the zone of proximal development. These three planning techniques are also ways to empower students to own and drive their own learning.

LOW FLOOR, HIGH CEILING TASKS

Although sometimes we need to assign learning activities with limited scope, we can often find ways to give our lessons and learning activities a low floor and a high ceiling. Low floor means that the task is accessible and there are some initial steps that all students can complete. All students can meaningfully engage and respond in some way. High ceiling means there are ways to take the activity in different directions and continue to do interesting work beyond the initial tasks. High ceiling means we ask students to do more than simply complete a clearly outlined task or answer a closed question.

In math, one of the ways to raise the ceiling is to teach students that any problem can be modeled in multiple ways. Students can learn that the primary purpose of solving word problems is not to race to the one right answer, but to find a variety of ways to represent and model the problem. We can teach students to look for similarities and connections between various models. We can also teach them to generate their own questions based on the scenario or problem of the day.

Writing projects often have low floor, high ceiling dimensions naturally built in. When students respond to engaging, open-ended prompts, they can use writing strategies that they've already solidified while also trying out new techniques. We can use graphic organizers, speech-to-text apps, and sentence stems as entry points to ensure all students are accessing the assignment.

To foster high ceiling writing projects, we can encourage students to apply all the writing strategies they know, to read their own work, and to identify places to revise. We can create an expectation that whenever students finish a draft, they can choose to revise and rewrite a previous piece, or they can choose to start a new piece.

Creating low floor, high ceiling projects is something to consider when planning a specific playlist, but it's also something to consider when planning the culture of your learning community. How do we teach students early in the year what to do if they finish one part of a playlist?

CHOICE AND VOICE

When students are given choices and are also given opportunities to share their unique voices, they are not only motivated to complete learning tasks, but they also become confident, self-directed participants in their own learning. Here's an illustration of this level of student engagement in action.

It was the third day of second grade. Molly's class had watched two videos about neurons, dendrites, and synapses, learning about how the brain changes as it learns. Molly's teacher, Mrs. Carpenter, drew a neuron on the board and introduced the second graders to the concept of creating a model. She pointed to the Create a Model core thinking skill poster and explained how a model needs to be accurate and include labels. "A drawing is one type of model," she said.

Mrs. Carpenter then explained to the students that they would create a model of two neurons, modeling how learning happens in the brain between the two neurons. As a class, they listed some tools available in their classroom that they might use to create their models. They listed markers, pipe cleaners, and Play-Doh. Mrs. Carpenter said, "What about Minecraft? Can we use Minecraft to make models?" Molly's whole face lit up. She and her classmates had used Minecraft as a learning tool in first grade, but she also loved to play at home. She couldn't wait to build her model.

For the next twenty minutes, students created their models. Molly's 3D model of two neurons inside Minecraft included signs for the labels and an electricity block representing a synapse. She carefully copied the words dendrite, synapse, and neuron onto her digital signs.

She was proud of her work and excited to log in to her school Minecraft account that evening to show her parents her model. She explained to them how synapses, the connections between neurons, get stronger when we learn and practice new skills. Other students took home Play-Doh and pipe cleaner models with handwritten labels.

Giving students choice and voice in their learning creates engagement and motivation. There are times, of course, when we want all students to write a paragraph with a specific structure or use a specific feature of a digital tool. When we ask all of our students to do the same thing at the same time in the same way, our purpose is usually to ensure that initial instruction is solidified, that students have a guided opportunity to practice an isolated skill. But as they acquire proficiency with a set of skills and strategies, we want students, even our youngest students, to make their own decisions. They need to practice selecting which strategy or tool fits their goals.

There are two main variables to look at when planning learning that includes more student choice. First, we can provide multiple ways for students to demonstrate content mastery. For example, after drafting a two-paragraph script about how an animal's adaptations help it survive in a specific habitat, students could choose to record their script as a presentation with audio that plays along to a series of images. Or they could record themselves presenting the information, like a short video documentary. We can also design assignments and learning activities that provide more choice by giving students the chance to choose their own topics. In the animals and habitats unit, for example, students could choose which animal to investigate.

PLAN AND TEACH TOWARD INDEPENDENCE

We design playlists around the Gradual Release of Responsibility model, with each skill and strategy building toward increasing levels of student proficiency, ownership, and responsibility. We are aiming for students who can independently select from and use a variety of strategies as they carry out projects focused on building the six core thinking skills that we'll talk more about in chapter four.

The Gradual Release of Responsibility model is a way to think about the levels of responsibility of the teacher versus the students in a lesson or in a series of lessons. At one end of the scale, teachers assume most of the responsibility, as they lecture or provide direct instruction. A focus lesson, mini-lesson, or think aloud are examples of this type of learning. This is when a teacher explicitly models a specific strategy or skill, and will often include the teacher thinking out loud, modeling the thinking and choices that students will eventually internalize.

Students begin to assume more responsibility during Guided Instruction. This is when teachers provide cues, prompts, and questions as students try out the new skill or strategy. Collaborative Learning is when students work together, supporting one another as they apply the skill or strategy. And finally, when students have fully mastered a skill or strategy, they can practice and use it independently (Fisher, et al., 2016).

In a playlist, the Focused Instruction and demonstrations can be short videos. Teachers can record themselves, use videos recorded by colleagues, or use the wealth of resources available online to curate a series of videos that explain concepts and demonstrate skills. The benefits of videos, opposed to live lessons, are that students can monitor their own learning needs and choose to pause and take notes, rewind the video to have content repeated, or rewatch the entire video.

Short quizzes with immediate feedback and active learning responses such as notes and drawings are two ways to embed guided practice in digital playlists. Turn-and-talk opportunities can also be part of a playlist. These can be in the form of instructions in the middle of a video to pause and talk to a partner, or as specific collaborative routines that students learn to follow as they work through a playlist with a partner. With two devices, for example, a pair of students can watch demonstration videos on one screen and work together to make the demonstrated product on the second screen.

Students can also record and submit short videos demonstrating their developing knowledge and skills. Playlists emphasize student reflection by including fillable forms with reflection prompts. A student might reflect on their mastery at the beginning and end of a specific playlist, with prompts about the academic content and about the core thinking skills that the playlist includes. This type of regular reflection encourages metacognition and self-direction.

SUMMARY

The primary vehicle we use to integrate digital tools into project-focused lessons and units are playlists. Playlists are versatile and flexible. They can be edited and adapted for different classes and for individual students. They can also be shared widely between teachers in a building, between schools in a district, and between teachers from different states and even countries. Playlists help build digitally integrated, project-focused classrooms where all students are continuously becoming self-directed, expert learners.

REFLECTION QUESTIONS:

Which lessons, units, or projects have you already moved into a digital format?_____

_____

_____

What are some of the ways you support students as they learn to work through video content and monitor their own learning?

_____

_____

_____

Consider the last time you needed to learn a new skill for a hobby or for a home project. How did you learn the skill? If you watched a video, did you watch it from beginning to end the first time through? Did you pause and try a small step? _____

_____

_____

REFERENCES

Fisher, D., Frey N., & Hattie, J. (2016). *Visible learning for literacy, grades k–12: Implementing the practices that work best to accelerate student learning.* Corwin Press.

Tucker, C. (2020, November 7). Blended learning: building a playlist. *Dr. Caitlin Tucker. https://catlintucker.com/2020/11/building-a-play-list/*

CHAPTER 4

The Six Core Thinking Skills

W E'VE DESCRIBED PLAYLISTS AS AN instructional tool to plan and organize a series of learning experiences. Although a playlist can be a series of activities for a single day of class time, they can also span several days and can include an end product or project.

Projects are loosely defined in our framework as any type of learning experience that gives students the opportunity to actively practice at least one of the six core thinking skills: Ask Questions, Build New Knowledge, Create Models, Communicate with Others, Conduct Experiments, and Design Solutions.

One of the biggest downfalls of the formal PBL (project-based learning) movement has been the high wall of intimidating jargon that gives educators the impression that planning effective projects involves a checklist of rarely obtainable features. Does your project solve a real-world problem? Is there an authentic audience? Does it integrate multiple subjects? Occasionally? Yes. Usually? No.

Let's use another baseball metaphor. A big, three-week project with an authentic outside audience that solves a real-world problem while integrating multiple subjects is like playing in the World Series. We might get there once per year, but we don't play in the World Series every day. We don't even play a real game against an opposing team every day.

Our daily work is showing up for practice. In baseball, this means batting drills, fielding practice, and getting with a single partner to throw the ball back and forth, playing a calm round of catch. This daily practice prepares players for the variety of situations that may arise in a game.

In our classrooms, the equivalent of daily practice is drafting, tinkering, and toying with new techniques and strategies. It looks like working together as a class to model and solve a challenging math problem, sharing our representations and computation strategies as we work.

Daily practice might also look like a focus lesson on a new writing technique that students are invited to apply in their own drafts immediately. It looks like engineering challenges and small, hands-on science experiments.

Sometimes a handful of lessons are aimed at creating a single product that integrates multiple subjects, but we often have subject-specific playlists and lessons that only carry through a single lesson or through a few days. Throughout each day, as students practice and become more skilled with each of the core thinking skills, we help them understand that practice is inherently valuable. We are doing important, valuable work whenever we practice and grow stronger thinking skills.

We also emphasize how the six core thinking skills cross subject boundaries. The process skills in the problem-solving cycle show up in math, writing, and science. Creating effective models is a skill that transfers into all disciplines. Students are more empowered as learners when they see how their daily work leads to skills that are useful in different subjects and can be activated to pursue their own goals.

Let's dive into each of the six core thinking skills.

Ask Questions

Asking questions is a fundamental skill that is an important part of each of the other six thinking skills. Student generated questions are the heartbeat of a learner-centered, project-focused classroom. One kindergarten teacher starts a new notebook each year titled "Our Questions," which she uses to jot down student questions whenever they arise. Here are a few of the kindergartners' questions.

"Why is there more than one planet?"

"Do fossils have DNA in them?"

"Is 30 odd?"

"How many atoms are in my hand?"

Although she won't be able to help students find answers to every question, by constantly recording their questions, this teacher is showing her learners how much she values questions and the individual ideas of each student.

Educators will recognize some learning strategies we use to help students hold fast to their early childhood habit of asking lots of questions. When we introduce a topic, we often use a KWL chart to have students list what they Know and Wonder before diving into new information and experiences. The L column is where we keep track of things we've Learned.

Questions are central to the Design Solutions and Conduct Experiments thinking skills. Questions are the launch pad and also the testing chamber. What are we going to build or make? What do we predict? What did we learn? Although we don't classify questions as "good" and "bad," we can encourage students to ask deeper and more productive questions by starting with "why" and "how," and teaching students to investigate underlying structures while considering impact.

In language arts, we teach students to ask questions when they use reading strategies such as predicting, visualizing, and inferring. In upper grades, the Notice & Note model (Beers, 2013) is an excellent way to help form habits of critical thinking while reading both fiction and non-fiction texts. In this model, students learn to ask specific questions when they encounter common signposts while reading.

For example, when reading fiction, if a character acts in a way that is unexpected, a student pauses and asks, "Why would the character do that?" We teach students that thinking about possible answers to this question can lead to strong predictions and might also help develop a deeper understanding of the book's themes.

An ambitious goal, which we encourage in all classrooms, is filling the room with more student-generated questions than teacher-generated questions. Curiosity and wonder are palpable in classrooms where students are constantly asking questions.

Build New Knowledge

By including Build New Knowledge as one of the core thinking skills, we hope to send students the clear message that they are in the driver's seat of mastering new knowledge. Students of all ages need to understand their own control over many subskills that can help them learn about new topics. They need a solid bank of strategies they can employ to acquire new knowledge efficiently and effectively.

Here is a list of some of these skills students need to be explicitly taught and then practice often.

Notice unfamiliar words in videos, in books, on websites, and in conversations
Use context cues to learn the meaning of new words
Use a variety of resources to find definitions of unknown words

Organize ideas and information into concept maps
Annotate texts
Make and use your own study notes—try both Sketch Notes and
    Cornel notes
Master specific study strategies such as self-quizzing
Understand how to most effectively space study sessions

We can also teach students that our understanding of both words and concepts becomes solid when we actively apply and use them. We might learn the phases of the moon, for example, by reading, watching videos, and taking notes. Yet we will have a far better understanding of the phases of the moon when we create and explain our own model that demonstrates how the light from the sun is reflected off the moon and back to earth to create each phase.

Create Models

Similar to Ask Questions, Create Models is a thinking skill that shows up everywhere. We use visual models to explain data using charts and graphs. Maps are models of physical spaces and can be used to understand the layout of a bedroom, a city, or the solar system. We can use diagrams to model the life cycle of a butterfly, a subatomic nuclear reaction, or the standard algorithm for subtraction. A family tree is a model of our ancestors, and a Venn diagram can be a model of how informational text is sometimes structured.

Models are powerful metaphors that both develop and shape our understanding of the world. In the younger grades, we teach students that models are accurate and have clear labels. In the older grades, we ask students to explain their models. We also teach them to describe the limits and assumptions of their models.

Models show up in several of the other core thinking skills. The skills to create and evaluate models can be the primary focus of a lesson or of a series of activities. Building models can also be integrated into lessons that are focused on other thinking skills as they are used to share information, plan solutions, map stories, or explain data.

Design Solutions

This thinking skill is based on the engineering and design processes. Engineers identify and define problems, imagine and plan solutions, and then create, test, and improve their inventions. From kindergarten through sixth grade, students learn the process as these five steps, which form a cycle that loops back on itself during each iteration of improvement.

ASK – IMAGINE – PLAN – CREATE – IMPROVE

When students become proficient with the steps of this process, they can transfer their persistence, creativity, and problem-tackling skills into many other settings, including non-academic situations. We can use the problem-solving cycle to solve any type of problem.

Although sometimes relegated to a weekly STEM class, all teachers can plan and teach STEM challenges and design learning activities that use the engineering process. Even if there isn't a direct tie-in to a content topic, engineering challenges build a vital thinking skill and are worth an hour of weekly class time. Students love having the chance to imagine, create, and improve their own inventions.

When the problem-solving cycle becomes an embedded part of a classroom culture, students are more likely to see mistakes as "perfect failures" and to value diverse perspectives. They are more likely to brainstorm solutions and try out creative new approaches. They become less likely to wait for help and more willing to tackle challenges on their own.

There is a plethora of online resources to find engineering projects. Google STEM challenges, makerspace, or engineering for kids. But be careful not to get lost in the rabbit holes of the internet. The goal is to have a lot of tinkering and trials, not to have perfect lessons or perfect products. Building boats and doing egg drops once each year are great ways for students to grow their engineering skills. But we also need to give students more frequent opportunities to build and create.

One teacher we know had a daily routine that she first implemented remotely and then continued when her students returned to in-person learning. Each student had one container of Play-Doh and a small set of plastic modeling blocks. Each day the students were given a five-minute engineering challenge. After building on their own or in pairs, the class spent a few minutes noticing and complimenting each other's work. This daily practice was vital to the positive class culture that transcended virtual and in-person settings.

Yes, we'll need solid classroom routines to independently manage materials. We'll need to plan routines for easy access, storage, and fast clean-up. We'll have some engineering projects and lessons that land better than others. And in the noise and mess, we'll likely wonder if it's worth the effort. It is. Students who learn and have many opportunities to practice the problem-solving cycle will develop the skills and mindsets of expert, independent learners.

Communicate With Others

All students need to develop effective writing, speaking, and communication skills. Digital tools can help students tell stories in ways that are beyond their current writing abilities. Students can record video and audio, applying speaking techniques that they will eventually apply to their writing. A slide presentation with audio recordings can hold the beginning, middle, and end of a story, or it can expand to include slides for each description and event.

In most classrooms, we have some students for whom the task of writing multiple sentences is beyond daunting. What digital recording tools can capture their ideas while their writing skills continue to grow?

Although narrative writing based on students' own experiences and memories is valuable, there are also many ways to integrate narrative writing into science and social studies units. Students can write diaries from the perspective or historical figures in social studies or from the perspective of an animal in science. Students can write scripts and record movies about dinosaurs, volcanoes, or revolutionary war heroes. Adding a story strengthens persuasive writing and brings informative writing to life.

We want all students to develop the ability to write informative and persuasive pieces that cite sources and integrate ideas. Yet we also want students to flexibly include pictures, audio clips, and video clips as they experiment with a variety of ways to share information.

A letter to the governor is one way to advocate for change. A viral meme or video is another way. By integrating digital creation tools into our writing units and lessons, we empower students to share information in ways that are aligned with the media-rich environment of the 2020s.

As we plan and teach projects that present information, it's helpful to remember that drafts and partially completed work are not only allowed, but encouraged. During a three-week unit on a specific science or social studies topic, for example, we might start off with two days of building new knowledge, followed by two or three days of building models, designing solutions, and conducting research. We'll conclude by creating small presentations to share the results of our models, inventions and/or research.

Just like artists fill their studios with hundreds of sketches, learners develop the ability to communicate effectively by trying out multiple techniques and by developing strong process skills. A publishing party or a polished, finished product once every eight weeks is a great goal. In the meantime, teach students to value the process of drafting and revising and to recognize their individual growth as writers, artists, and as learners who can share information in engaging, effective ways.

Conduct Experiments

We want all students to develop the ability to think like scientists. This includes a host of skills connected to the scientific method, including predicting, analyzing, observing, measuring, reporting, and classifying.

Although we want students to understand the big picture of the scientific process, we can also focus our lessons on one or two of these subskills at a time. We can ask students to analyze a set of data, to classify rocks, or to represent the results of simple experiments. How many drops of water fit on the face of a penny? What brand of paper towel is strongest when wet? What is the range of heights of the students in our class?

Although we want to keep the daily work manageable, we also want students across the elementary grades to understand the entire process of designing and conducting an experiment. We can scaffold and coach younger students through the steps of a whole experiment as we emphasize the purpose of using the scientific method. Even our youngest students can learn precise academic words like variable, hypothesis, and analyze.

SUMMARY

Each day, as students do the actual work of writers, engineers, artists, and scientists, they become actively engaged with the world of ideas. They also grow the specific knowledge, skills, and mindsets of our home-plate outcomes. Students in a project-focused classroom see learning as an active, exciting process, and they come to see themselves as skilled learners who can successfully and independently acquire new knowledge and skills and solve challenging problems.

REFLECTION QUESTIONS

Why might learning and understanding the six core thinking skills be important for students? _____
_____
_____
_____

How is the "Ask – Imagine – Plan – Create – Improve" cycle already part of your classroom or part of your own creative process as an instructional designer? _____
_____
_____

What would a rubric or learning progression for one of the core thinking skills look like for your learners? _____

_____

_____

_____

REFERENCES

Beers, K., & Probst, R. E. (2013). *Notice and note strategies for close reading.* Heinemann.

CHAPTER 5

Data-Informed Innovation

CREATING CLASSROOMS IN WHICH STUDENTS are highly self-directed and able to work independently through digital lessons is often a daunting challenge for teachers. Yet because of the pandemic, we have become more proficient with many digital tools that can support this shift. Our challenge is to design classrooms and schools that take advantage of these tools while also giving each student the in-person coaching and the supportive social environment that so many students went without for more than a full school year.

SELF-DIRECTION

To implement the Dugout framework, we suggest that teachers set aside at least one time period each day for self-direction. During these blocks of time, students work through playlists, and they also work on adaptive digital platforms or other independent activities, such as reading side-by-side with a peer.

In kindergarten, first, and second grade, self-direction can be built into small group rotations. At the beginning of the year, each independent routine is carefully and explicitly modeled and practiced.

When they introduce a routine, teachers list desired behaviors and give students many opportunities to practice the routines correctly, building a sense of student ownership.

After a few weeks of guided practice and encouragement students are able to manage their own attention, materials, and behaviors during sustained periods of independence. As students reach the middle and upper elementary grades, this same attention to independent routines can be used to create learning cultures in which students are able to self-direct for large chunks of the day.

Self-direction is not only a chance for students to foster the Dugout mindsets of agency and growth as they drive their own learning, but while students are engaged in self-directed activities, teachers are able to teach small groups and support individual student needs.

When you are planning the first month of school, think about routines that will address the following parts of a self-direction block: accessing and storing devices, appropriate help-seeking strategies, transitions, and collaborative work. Solid routines save time and create a classroom culture where students know what to do and what to expect.

The appropriate amount of whole class versus digital instruction will vary widely across grades and depend on the needs of each class. Yet, in general, the role of the teacher in this model shifts as there is less time spent on whole-class instruction and more time spent supporting students through individual and small-group coaching sessions.

DIGITAL CREATION TOOLS

In order for students to effectively work through digital playlists, students need a small set of digital creation tools that they can use independently. The specific tools depend on your local context. Are you an Apple school or a Microsoft district? What tools have students used in prior grades?

Most digital tools on the market today can be effectively used with students. The process of learning the features and becoming proficient with a new digital tool is valuable regardless of the brand or company. Students will have countless occasions to learn new digital tools throughout their lives. Here are some examples of digital creation tools.

> *Presentation Tools: Microsoft PowerPoint, Apple Keynote, Google Slides*
> *Video Tools: iMovie, Flipgrid, Microsoft Stream*
> *Modeling Tools: Minecraft, Scratch, and green screen apps*

Starting in third grade, we also teach and use a word processing tool. In either fourth or fifth grade, students learn how to use a spreadsheet program with data analysis tools. Although elementary schools often have a weekly class devoted to computer and technology skills, it's also important that classroom teachers master and feel comfortable teaching and integrating these tools directly into daily learning activities. If we have a weekly computer class, we can coordinate lessons to teach digital creation tools. One lesson per week, however, will not be enough. Students will need more time to practice and experiment with the tools.

THE PLAN-DO-CHECK-ADJUST CYCLE

There is not one right way to implement the Out of the Dugout model. With a clear vision of the home plate outcomes, we take things one unit, one student, and one day at a time.

As we move to providing more time in which students are working on their own, as they learn and practice new content and skills through playlists and on adaptive platforms, we can use the Plan-Do-Check-Adjust Cycle to ensure that each student is learning. This is a cycle of innovation and gradual improvement that we can apply to a single lesson, a unit of study, or to our overall implementation of self-direction blocks (Laub, 2021).

The first step of the Plan-Do-Check-Adjust Cycle is to plan the lesson, the unit, or the series of focus lessons and guided practice that students will learn. Don't plan alone. Use your colleagues or online peers to find what has worked. Consider recording short teaching videos and sharing them with others. The vulnerability of seeing ourselves on screen is real. But the benefits of using videos to teach—and sharing our instructional videos and playlists with others—are worth it. As you design playlists, include scaffolds, learning progressions, and formative checks.

The next step of the Plan-Do-Check-Adjust Cycle is to do it. Carry out the plan. Set a personal goal to step back and let students struggle through the challenges of becoming more independent. Give it time and consider the specific support or goals each student might need to become more independent and self-directed.

Next, evaluate how things are going. Look at student work as a primary source of data and also ask for a colleague or school administrator to observe the class during self-direction. Classrooms are incredibly complex environments and the more eyes and information we can get, the better. Let observers know that self-direction doesn't need to be silent, but we want to know if students are supporting one another in productive ways, and what students do when they get stuck.

The final step, before starting the cycle again, is to adjust. As we look at our evidence of student learning and review our observations, we can refer back to the home plate to evaluate how things are going. Are students building new knowledge and skills? How do we know? What can we change to foster more learning and more independence? Are there routines that we need to reteach and practice? Are students engaged in the authentic work of scientists, engineers, writers, and scholars? What do small groups and individual students need next?

One of the most insightful lessons we observed as school administrators was during a self-direction block in a fourth-grade class. Pairs of students were spread around a classroom, most sitting at low tables or on the floor. The kids were excitedly working inside Minecraft worlds. They were giving each other suggestions and support. One pair was also talking about recess issues and their plans for after school.

At the side of the room, the teacher was completely focused on the four students who were sitting at her table. They were reviewing a math concept on small white boards. She didn't seem to see or notice the noise or the behaviors of the other students.

When we talked to the teacher later, she shared data that showed all of her students had achieved their learning goals that day. She explained how hard it had been when she first implemented a self-direction block. It had felt loud and messy and uncomfortable. But she stuck with it for several months and saw her students making strong academic progress, while also becoming more independent, engaged, and confident.

SUMMARY

As we use the Plan-Do-Check-Adjust Cycle each week in our professional learning communities and to inform our decisions as instructional designers, we can create effective routines and playlists. By thoughtfully adding to and subtracting from the lessons and routines we've used in the past, we will gradually build digitally integrated, project-focused classrooms. We will build classrooms and schools where students are always out of the dugout, where they are constantly rounding the bases of learning, and where they each slide into home plate as empowered, expert learners.

REFLECTION QUESTIONS

What are the digital creation tools that your students will learn and use throughout the year?_____
_____
_____

Which lessons or units can be most readily be moved into a playlist format?_____
_____
_____
_____

What will your Plan-Do-Check-Adjust Cycle look like? Who are your peers that will give you the support you need to engage in a process of data-informed innovation? _____
_____
_____
_____
_____

REFERENCES

Laub, J. (2021, June 10). Lean Education Tools. *https:/https://www. leanthink.org/education-tool*

LOOKING FOR MORE?
CHECK OUT

WWW.OUTOFTHEDUGOUT.COM

Made in the USA
Middletown, DE
22 August 2022

70946305R00033